BURNING
MY BIRTH
CERTIFICATE

BURNING
MY BIRTH
CERTIFICATE

Poems

Pamela Sutton

THE ASHLAND POETRY PRESS

Printed in the United States of America

ISBN: 978-0-912592-81-7

LCCN: 2017959417

Cover art: *Sunset on the Plains* by Albert Bierstadt, courtesy of Spencer Museum of Art, University of Kansas, gift of Charles Kincaid in honor of his wife, Edith Kincaid, 1961.0006.

Cover design: Nicholas Fedorchak

Acknowledgments & Notes

The author gratefully acknowledges the following publications who published early versions of the poems in this book.

The American Journal of Poetry, forthcoming "Big Tree, USA"
Prairie Schooner, "Organic Mask" and forthcoming "Burning My Birth Certificate" and
       "Afraid to Pray"
American Poetry Review, "World Without Glass," "Gnat Season," "Today's Nudes" and
       "Love, and a Bit With a Dog"

For Mabel Clifford McDaniel

Contents

"Most of my symphonies are tombstones."
—*Shostakovich*

Plainsong Rain

When a singular voice
Blends into plainsong rain
I feel clean and whole.
I want to begin again.

How did I find your instructions
To build a sanctuary of wet leaves?

Primitive, Equine

The towers falter impossibly and implode. A team of muscular Clydesdales breaks loose from their harnesses and tackle. As in a waking Guernica nightmare I chase the giant, panicked horses all over the Kentucky farm. My boots slip over and over in muddy vermilion clay. My palms blister then bleed from sodden rope. Their silvery feathers redden with mud from hoof head to fetlock. Their necks arch and spring high and away like oblique bridges breaking. But I must catch and calm the horses because in their frenzied terror they could become deadly. Horse power. Hooves like mason's mallets kick out at me. Blinding-bright squares of rain flood the farm as I rope one horse, only to lose another. Blue-black sky pours reams of sparkling hand-written opera. I spin in erratic circles trying to catch the soaked pages as they crumble into my hands like papier mache. Horses and rope and opera. Tornadic Clydesdales. Ears laid flat against their heads; intelligent eyes wide and white with lightning; broad hooves kicking out at me, and within the darkest depths of me: primitive, equine. Wet music falling; never caught and collected. Never silenced; never heard.

World without Glass (after 9/11)

This is not,
beloved daughter,
the world I roughed-out for you—
world without glass:
all windows shattered;
all mirrors broken;
bad luck forever.

We are left only with stone. And names.
Aethelstan sounds like Afghanistan;
"stone" sounds like "stan."
And "stan" means "place."
If the stones ever cease to bleed,
I beg you wipe them clean
and learn to read
the first idea of heaven:
Skara Brae; the Stones of Steness;
Sunkenkirk; and Stonehenge.
Enter into that ampitheatre
and worship rocks an astronaut
stole from the moon—there:
"between the woods and frozen lake
the darkest evening of the year."
Worship the feldspar and spotted dolorite;
the green-stone and blue-stone.
And from these stones learn how to write.

Having no glass, we are reduced to narrow
open windows and violent weather.
Therefore, make much of the light.
Braid the stone. Be certain
to carve your Letters out
rather than pounding them in. Though
more difficult, your words will be hypnotic.
The future will clamor
to place hands upon your story

about how we once had
a world with glass:
the crystalline morning we thought was ours—
and how it burst
into broken wings and desert wars.

What I Want from the Hand-Built Log Cabin on Lac du Flambeau Indian Reservation, Which You Sold for No Good Reason

Mail me the bus-sized boulder
that could never be moved
by dynamite or bulldozer.

Send the owl's midnight question:
"Who's there? Who's there?"

Fed Ex all the Ojibway dances—
their drums re-threading each bead
of my blood into a dream-catcher.

Email the smell of knotty pine.
Twitter the iridescent hummingbirds
jousting for nectar.

Box up the sound of the aluminum canoe
cutting through rough current and glass.
Throw in the patterns of water-spiders
walking upon the still water.

Send the quiet stones; each full moon;
and every sun that ever set
on White Sand Lake.

Don't forget to Overnight the loon's weeping
and the eagle's height at noon.

Above all, Express mail the thickest log dad ever split:
so thick he had to fling it backwards over
his shoulder then heft it forwards onto
the chopping block again and
again and over and over until
the dense core cracked

in half; then fourths;
then eighths; then kindling.
I am a lost child alone
in a black metal forest sharp and cold:
black because gone, because sold.

Send fire.

Looking for Ray

Spinning a mirror between my palms
the word "brave"
the word "man"
twirling faster, faster seeing
a face and the words "brave man."

Banner of smoke unfurls like Batman's cape
over Gotham City. Then the sinking
feeling of floors collapsing—
doors opening to clouds,
to reams of bright paper—
confetti nightmare parade;
ninety interlocking stories
melting beneath my feet;
tectonic plates sheering the ocean floor,
wrestling the God be-deviled sky,
dropping through gloves of liquid metal,
grabbing doorknobs locked forever,
climbing staircases spiraling
through windows shredding light,
holding the incandescent words
"brave man" "brave man"
torching the air from my lungs,
branding the heart in my hands;
landing in the twisted sheets
of my soft, warm bed
that will never feel safe again.

Looking for Ray in the cereal aisle
of the supermarket.
Still looking.
Looking for Ray.

Bhutan Archer

Count the waterfalls soaring like infinite
arrows over Taroko Gorge.

I embrace each sharp child.

Make hideous the pageantry of war,
which is not lovely. War is not
a red cardinal marching among
white blossoms.

My father was a soldier;
his father was a soldier;
his father was a soldier.
Get the point?

Bhutan archer! Splinter my tears
into fletched ocean waves.

Set each wave on fire.

Gnat Season

One brown gnat scuttles between letters on this page;
a second draws a dotted line across the inside of my wrist:
cut along the dotted line....
And now I see a whole tribe floating in my coffee.
Why do they die just to ruin my skinny vanilla latte?

It is South Florida's season of brown gnats, and I hate
the season of brown gnats. Their ochre-bald heads turn up
to look at me and my visceral rage at their tenacity.
They are only the size of Lincoln's eye on a penny
or the dot over the letter "i." Killing them all would
cleanse the world forever of dirt sewn in sweaty broadcloth.

But I choose not to kill them. They are silent and do not bite.
Their population is their pestilence: one of me; billions of them.
From here each gnat looks like a perfectly cut scarab—
oily diamonds spilling from one place to another.

They gather on this page as if to codify an urgent message:
something about coffee or coffee-brown dung water:
something about thirst greater than the fear of death.

Today's Nudes (Uffizi Gallery, Florence)

are nothing like yesterday's nudes
surfing on an open shell blown in by Zephyrs.
Melancholy ripens in her pearlescent gaze. She
knows the flowers tossed in celebration at her feet today
will be buried with her tomorrow.

Today's nudes are nothing
like the Sabine women rising up from an
800-year-sleep of chiseled outrage. Marble muscles
twist awake in the Florentine sun.

Today's nudes appear and vanish at Google-speed.
Satellites lasso and tether a blindfolded woman in a circus pose.
See the red rubber ball stuffed in her mouth
and strapped tightly in place around her head.
See her suspended in mid-air like a female piñata.

Or, today's nudes are erased from head to toe in chador;
then buried to the neck in sand whittled from the coldest stars.
Watch the hand-thrown stones sculpt her face, instead of
the other way 'round.

Tolkien's Lost Chapters

What if I found them
neatly prepared in hand-
written notebooks; or just
shadows of words stained
autumn leaves on wet sidewalks? —

among lost students
for whom I gave my life
centuries ago while
steering three-masted Dutch ships
pulled by orange bulbous sails lit
like paper lanterns like
rows of papier-mache skulls
in which floated the compass of history —

What if I found
Tolkien's lost chapters
in children's brains blown
to barnacles—to binnacles
by suicide bombers,

when all I was looking for
was my whole heart,
my lost country,
my English Department office?

The Mouse Lemur

is the smallest primate on the planet.
Not even the size of my thumb,
its bat-like ears are thin as skin

I peel after a sunburn.
The Mouse Lemur stares through me
with eyes red and round as bullet holes:

O crooked moon—O bloody syzygy
balancing the Madagascar dusk.
In Malagasy, which is a lot like Hawaiian—

the language of Paradise—
"Lemur" means "spirits of the dead."
The wounds wedged into a child's torso

read like cuneiform. And the pre-
historic alleys of Aleppo rock to and
fro with hell-fire laser-guided missiles.

A mother wipes the tears of her shrapnel-
pocked son. She says:
"I will murder the Alawites with my teeth."

The Mouse Lemur catches a moth
in its finger-tips. Puffs of bitten wing
throw powder into the air.

Organic Mask

I was taught that if evolution was a ladder,
we, being human, had climbed the highest rung;
or, if evolution was a tree,
we, being hominid, had climbed the farthest down
and away, until our ambition—prehensile, australopithecine—
flowed over the planet and froze like black, vitreous lava;
until we pronounced the language of the forest
with the metal teeth of cacophonous saws;
until we had constructed a warehouse from a temple.

In the nocturnal mammal section of the Philadelphia Zoo,
the Slow Loris greets me with eyes grown huge
from eons of accommodating darkness.
With vestigial limbs—branches of flesh—
he trundles through the artificial biotope toward me.
Each step is a twisting-off from the tree
where specialization nailed him down to stay.
As if to frame my face, pressed against the glass,
he places rudimentary hands upon the window
and looks at me with the organic mask of God.

Burning My Birth Certificate

Her bones are buried deep in the garden
near her favorite window where she watched
the birds and the black-
red winter roses. I am burning
my birth certificate. I am pouring the ashes
over her grave.

Last April I carried her body home
through green-black rain—wet knuckles
punching my face and shoulders,
but she had to be buried, and it was only me.

The earth was still thawing, the storm was a boxer
who out-weighed me, over-muscled me and my
shovel and boots. I still can't stand to wear
the boots—clay stuck to their soles.

They are good boots, the best, and the shovel
well made. They were bought to plant tulips
not dig a grave, and never to dig one for her.

Placing her body in that eye-socket of earth
was like handing over my heart—only
bone now, and a bit of hair. I stare
out of Pearl's favorite window and see

all the lost animals all over this war-pocked
skull of a planet. I see all
the children's dead pets; the bombs
planted over and over
in houses like mine. I see
my child's dead pet. I see
lost horses trotting and dying and rotting;
dogs forming packs; and the children who loved them.

Night Mowing

I like to mow my lawn at night;
moon's lid squeezed tightly
over my shoulder to the right.

I like to mow my lawn in the dark
amphibian kingdoms
I blindly slaughter down.

Sliced gecko fingers stick to the blades.
And now I think the grass
is the beautiful uncut hair of un-marked graves.

Wild flowers shaped like kettles
—once upon a time a schtetl. I smell
like sweat and blood and metal.

My muscles ache from beetle battle.
And now I think grass is the bluntly
sheared hair of a civilization.

My push-mower rattles like a Tommy-gun,
but when the regimen is done,
the sky sprouts stars like marigolds,

which I may never cut nor hold.

Half Notes

"Black they all were, with the sweet, noble black of Africa,
Deep darkness absorbed through an age, like old soot,
That makes you feel that for elegance, vigor and vivacity,
No color rivals black."
— *Isak Dinesen,* Out of Aftrica

From Africa's color-wheel, Dinesen loved best
the elegance of black feathers.
One morning she counted 47 hornbills—
half-notes sketched on a straight-branched acacia tree.

Rosa Parks died today,
but someone else died too:
Delois, my best boss,
I lift this poem to you.

This is the poem
I never wanted to write:
ink on paper is permanently
Black and White.

Whenever I made a mistake you said:
"There's nothing new under the sun.
Don't lose sleep. A new day's begun."

You must have known
I was raised on the N-word:
That it simmered like an egg frying
in the dark, iron skillet of my heart.
That it made an upstart's nest
in the green tree of my life.

Delois, when you died I stared
directly into the sun.
A solar flare sliced "nigger" out forever.
Hamlet knew, and so did you:
"better half a heart that's pure
than a whole heart that's corrupt."

Now I wander the streets of this City
of Brotherly Love blind-crazy,
lifting up the pruned, bloodied branches
of my heart in my hands,
crying: "Look Delois, look!:
Here's something new—
new under the sun."

"Big Tree, USA"

Fox Network typo for "bigotry in the USA"

*"Cherish your fantasy! . . . Don't let the Freudians coax it away
or the Pharmacists poison it out of you. Hold it dear, for when
you lose it you begin to cease to be."*
—"Dr. Hilarious" from Thomas
Pynchon's The Crying of Lot 49

The sky is blue and blousey
but there are no ladders.
Delois! I am still falling and you are still buried. Sometimes
I wish you had taken me with you.
Sometimes I wish I could leave you alone.
I'll bet you wish the same thing.
So, Delois: here's my latest report:
This morning's black, tropic thunder blasts
its heavy artillery through low clouds
baptizing my forehead.

What is the lightning planting?

Right now an un-manned drone shreds children like classified documents.
And now a 19-year-old Marine steps on an IED.

You were smart to die when you did, Delois.
Lightning rakes the true face of America.
It is monstrous. It is Grendel.
Rich and I met for dinner in Orlando.
We still miss you.
Rich takes 50 mg of Prozac; I take 60
of the North American sacrament.
It numbs us to the taste of muddy, third-world,
feces water and blinds us to the children drinking it right now.

I wonder why I'm still talking to you and if
you can hear me in your heaven.
Is heaven segregated? I didn't think so.
Say hello to Michael Jackson for me.

I wish you had lived to see the first half-Black President get elected.
For 24 hours the nation quaked ecstatic. Everything went Pentecostal:
For one brief day America was possessed with the Holy Spirit:
trembling, weeping, babbling in tongues only the dead could hear.
Did you hear me, Delois?
Did—You—Hear—Me?

Can you hear me now?
And can you hear the hate miners
drilling in the secret dark? Can you hear them harvesting
that vein of racist, Silurian coal? America has discovered
its endless supply of energy.

Delois, I thought the Civil War was over, but I think it's just getting started.

I speak to you, Delois, because I want to know what the dead are thinking.
I've heard what the living have to say and it is always: god and war and
god and war and god and war and god.

Delois I speak to this storm and hope your ears are the round
grapewood leaves flapping, catching my voice, singing it back to me, translated.
How I wish I'd stopped dead in the street at 6th & Pine
and given you a full hug on your way into Lippincott.
But it wouldn't have been professional. I pretended not to see you.
And that was the last time I ever saw you.
You gave me a good job and a good life for as long as possible.
You're the only one who ever did.

9/11 destroyed our company—the oldest publishing house in America: 1792.
We published *To Kill a Mockingbird* and Pynchon's *The Crying
of Lot 49*. Dr. Hilarious was right: "cherish your fantasy! . . . don't let the Freudians
coax it away or the pharmacists poison it out of you."

Do you laugh at the jokes I tell only you when I'm alone? —
which is always now. No one notices that I am falling; or hears that the wind
is my harrowing scream. And they are blind to my flailing arms grappling at sky.
They're all just walking around like everything's normal.
No one smells the acrid smoke billowing from my lips
or sees that I am on fire. No one reaches out to catch me.

Delois: It's springtime in Philadelphia.
Cherry blossoms and snow rush
to the cobbled streets. Twenty years ago, kicking up those petals
I felt anointed and certain that life would be good no matter what,
no matter where I worked, just walking through petals washing
the round stone paths of glory.

But the mockingbirds, Delois, the mockingbirds:
they're being slaughtered in Biblical numbers.

Women and children are being raped and starved right now
in this poem in Darfur;
We are still at war with Afghanistan.
Something is rotten in the state of Denmark now. It is monstrous,
it is Grendel X-treme and Supersize Grendel and Grendel multiplying
according to Moore's Law: every 18 months the microchip shrinks, and
Grendel grows.

I watched your son and mother carry away
a cardboard box of your office things.
9/11 killed us all in a way:
Sarah FitzHugh jumped off the Ben Franklin Bridge;
Rich started drinking;
I began listening to mockingbirds;
then I started talking back.
Now I am speaking to you:
to the Black, wise, dead who know what I could never have imagined.
And when I'm not speaking to you I am silent
and listening:

A mockingbird trills on the telephone wire above my rented yard.
His tiny throat bulges with the fierce urgency of now.
Maybe his song is pure language and ours the bad mimicry of
"ancient scar, ancient scar, ancient scar. . . ."
which we can only hear as "god and war;
god and war; god and war."

He might be warning of Apocalypse, now:
telling me what to pack, where to hide;
what kind of batteries, how many.

But all I hear is your voice — the deafening ocean of the universe.
And all I see is the Earth flying up fanning my business suit into flames.

Thirteen Ways of Looking at Martin Luther King Day

for Derek Walcott

1. Poetry is a balancing act on a burning I-beam
swaying a hundred stories above inferno.
A Caribbean poet sits on a throne at the far end
of the molten I-beam. He wears a fiery crown;
laughs, and coaxes me across.

2. Not black; not white: ash gray. Finally,
we are all the same color.

3. My sister and I fight over the backseat armrest
in Grandma's pink Cadillac. I win, and sit up high
on the narrow, cushioned throne, wearing paisley
culottes and yellow cat-eye sunglasses. 1966: South
Carolina: we pull into the Laundromat.
A sign says: "Whites only." Walking into the
Laundromat I blurt out: "Hey, if it's 'Whites Only' how
can we get all our clothes clean?"

4. Hutton Plantation: a room crowded with hunting trophies—
ibex and antelope thrust helical antlers towards Africa—
glass eyes stare through me at their own extinction.

5. Abandoned slave quarters: Butterfly eggs hatching
on wild raspberries: lids parting; eggshells blinking open
by worms that would have wings. Each abandoned egg is
a hardened skein of veins: microscopic urns where
worms were bound; butterflies, born.

6. A woman with fair skin orders a meal at a diner.
She has red hair, freckles, but is served stares, not food.
Dad whispers: "She has Negroid features." Dad has red
hair, freckles. I'm 6 years old. The diner's chrome flashing
vibrates with nausea—my first swallow of rancid knowledge.

7. Street person named "Paris." Each day he folds a crown of tin foil. Each day he draws paradise on the back of blueprints from the Savannah River Nuclear Power Plant. No one knows where he gets the blueprints, the chalk, the foil for crowns.

8. Now I dream of gardens—the heavy untamed gardens that can only be found in the deep South. I am a child running among the waxy thumbs of magnolia blossoms, my lungs thick with dense, pollinated air. Morning: the sun is hot; air is cold. Steam rises from the river. Saltwater meets fresh. My breath polishes sunlight the way glasses fog up on a cold morning; smell of Spanish moss. I'm racing toward a border of sculpted boxwood. The sun points downward like an arrow. Grandma is there, arms outstretched, holding a spherical garden clock out to me.

9. JFK. MLK. RFK. Lincoln Memorial.

10. B.B. King. Muddy Waters. Billie Holiday. Checkerboard Lounge.

11. Harper's Ferry: Walking through a cemetery to reach a cliff overlooking the violent convergence of rivers: Potomac and Shenandoah. John Brown inhales the subtle rage of flowers.

12. A group of toddlers cross an intersection in Philadelphia: black and white children holding hands. "Cherish your fantasy."

13. Poetry is a balancing act on a burning I-beam. A hundred stories above inferno. An old Caribbean poet rattles his crown at me like a tambourine: "You must grab hold to live." As I touch
his crown it folds into a tin-foil hat; a basketball hoop;
the rim of a trumpet; a noose of barbed wire;
"Shield of Achilles";
iris of God.

Angels

Have swarmed into poetry
camouflaged by a winter plumage
of white, membranous paper.

If you're a poet, forget it:
they'll mimic every gesture like an 8-year-old kid
you're stuck sitting next to on an eternal train ride.
You yawn, they yawn; you prop your face in your hands,
and so do they.

But I wonder, don't you, if they are more than
a 21st century Literary gimmick?
What if, after all, they are for real,
they aren't just kidding,
and they are stealthily invading the planet by way of poetry—
by way of ink so black it's white as a cape of feathered bone.

I have long since lost faith in God,
but I will never lose faith in angels
and their fulminant folding of the sky
into a tornado of ten-thousand snow geese
trumpeting over a winter field draped against the ocean.

They cannot decide whether to land
or fly in formation.
They cannot decide whether to turn into snow.
They spiral upward spelling a geometry of hope
they will never be able to translate
into one audible human word.

So they have migrated into poetry;
they have populated our city streets,
as poor and common,
black, bent, skinny as commas
that interrupt our breathing;
that interrupt our walking.

Especially the one who folds a crown of tin foil
for himself each day.
New crown; new day.
He spends time drawing a tropical Jesus
on sidewalks with pastel chalk.

When it snows wet snow, the vision melts.
And when the vision melts he draws paradise
on classified blueprints
from the Savannah River Nuclear Weapons Plant.

No one can guess where he gets the blueprints
or the chalk or the foil for crowns.
And no one believes him, of course,
when he says he's a messenger of Christ,
when he says he is Christ himself.
But I wonder, don't you,
if he's not just one of the poor, insane, dispossessed;
if he's not just kidding;
if the messenger has become the message;
if he's telling the truth.

Citizen

Fog smudges the outline of sun
like an eraser soiled with the folly of Dutch suns:
rubbed out as they rise.

I enter Anne Frank's house as a tourist,
at first relieved I'm not a Jew.
But ascending the stairs to her room
a burning swastika ratchet unzips my spine.

There is the basin where she washed;
there is where she stepped quietly in stocking feet—
and up there, that, is where she wrote.
Today the bells of Westertoren still tumble their songs
against a sky swollen shut with weeping.
My heart splits—
like the binding of a diary
knocked from a young writer's hand.

I exit onto the street along the canal
as a new citizen of that country where
the unbending will of light
illuminates each bead of fog.
Just touching the hem of her language,
I burn.

My Black Pearl

There is always the night.

Never mind that I chose the practical one:
a man with a job with a future—
marketable and multiply degreed,
from a family with money
and an echelon of antique clocks
ordering each hour forward.

There is always the night.

Never mind his attempts to locate and satisfy
that remote landscape inside me:
a boulder field resonates with hollow aching.
Never mind the ziggurat of accomplishments we call home,
nor the dying happiness I am able to resuscitate
by the end of each day.

There is always the night.

And like a planet collapsing in its own weight,
you still disturb within me
a small, hard husk of love that never flowered.
The more years I clam you up,
the more beautiful, more luminous you become—
my black pearl—

living on the West coast, I hear,
and climbing, always climbing
to reach the precipitous heights
required by everyone you've ever loved,
including me.

Could you forgive me if you knew
that I, on the East coast,
am deaf now to the wishes of others—
unable to sleep or to marry?

Rain in Guangzhou

"—Till elevators drop us from our day..."
—Hart Crane, "The Bridge"

At the New York board meeting they assured me our Chinese staff
at the 4-color printing plant are happy, dedicated workers;
that unity with Hong Kong has vastly improved their output,
their cost, their lives. They even get to live in the same building
where they work. And suddenly in the glass and mahogany boardroom
I'm riding a hovercraft 30 years ago up river from Hong Kong
into "Red" China. All day I floated on a pneumatic bubble
past gleaming high-rises, segmented junks, ferries, tugboats, and
cargo ships through Hong Kong harbor, back in time it seemed
a hundred years, past mud brick villages, water-buffalo plows,
sampans stuck together with reeds and dung, bad concrete attempts at
Modernization; not believing one thing I saw, even
as I disembarked the boat—army-issue green—
same color as the cinder-block government buildings and uniforms
the young people wore. Nor could I believe the tyrannical rain;
the mud pit I shit in daily; squatting gingerly.
Children's ribs protruded like harp-strings—if I thrummed them
what would I hear? Nor could I believe
the single light-bulb swaying from the ceiling—interrogation of light;
the damp towel I draped over my legs at night so I would not be
awakened by roaches and mice. Did I mention
the leaky restaurant and a waitress who carved a sampan
for me out of winter melon rind? Rain
in Guangzhou pierces like the singing
of a thousand captive birds.
Surely, they must be happier now,
living where they work, printing 4-color books:
just like the billboard I sped past 30 years ago in a dizzying sea of bicycles:
a robust proletarian declared: "Work is happiness"; hammer in hand.
Hadn't I heard something like this somewhere before?
Arbeit Macht Frei.
When I returned to Hong Kong from China it was still raining—
so heavy and dark that Asians pressed en masse along skyscrapers,

lifting their black umbrellas uniformly against the clouds. For once the sidewalks were empty. Free. I ran full speed, alone, through the downpour—palms catching sky.

The Last Supper

Rain
in Guangzhou   Pierces
like the   Singing
Of a thousand captive   Birds.

Hungry,
I ate at a restaurant with
a black and white checkered floor missing tiles,
a leaking roof and
a waitress named Aiwa.

Her face was born the color
of a wooden box
          and shaped as square
in which were cut
   Sparse sparrow eyes.

The edges of her sickle mouth
opened the box
When she smiled,
and she smiled as   One
                              Grateful for the good fortune of others.

She smiled at   My good fortune,
and served
   Rice wine, roast goose skin,
and many other delicacies.   She served but never tasted.
I carved
a sampan for her out of winter melon rind.
When she smiled
the box opened
my good fortune.

Her umbrella leaked
as she walked me to a bus.

She held the punctured section
over her own head, keeping mine dry.

Puddles washed my feet
where bricks were missing in the street.

Boxed,
inside the cool, dry bus,

I watched   Aiwa   Through the window as we drove away,
but when   She   Smiled
            My   good fortune
                   Opened the box
                   And I was
          Full.

Rain
in Guangzhou
       Pierces
               Like the   Singing
            Of a thousand   Captive   Birds.

Question for the End of the Century

If kisses were atonement for the rain;
If rain could turn to snow and melt again;
If I found you underneath a willow tree;
If a wet, Atlantic snow were cleansing me
And the city air and your weary curls—
Cupped in your open hands like jewels;
If wet snow wept upon my skin in fever;
If I still confused love with anger;
If, then, I turned to walk away from you
Toward the cold side of the year away from you;
If I started walking toward the end of the century
Away from you toward the end of this merciless century,
Would you ask me not to leave just once, again,
If kisses atoned for rain?

Aurora Borealis

for Vicki

We were seven we made plans
to meet after the grass fires lacquered the field
between our houses to a smooth black mirror.
The Midwest was supposed to be a safe place.
I still feel the soles of my P.F. Flyers melting.

It was 1967, before the Illinois prairie was ploughed
into suburbs and strip-malls. It was just
your house and mine and waves of smoke
for five days eclipsing the sun as our parents
hosed down   roofs   cars   lawns.   Our mothers
promised our homes would be spared

while the gorgeous fire blackened every modern thing—
Mustang   bird bath   bird house   Schwinn—
while the fire grabbed our peter pan collars
and held us up to the invisible ink of the wind
driving the smoke, the grass, the direction of the sun,
the inebriated sky swirling with liquid smoke denial—
alcohol and Valium, absence and rage.

We were ten we made maps made plans—
to run away run away run away run—
we hid in a tree-trunk hollowed out by lightning—
ate wild mulberries—sang Scarborough Fair—
breviary of small lips—lasted one day.

At Wisconsin summer camp we accepted Christ
as our personal Savior
during a sermon on the End Times
wedged between the Aurora Borealis
and a campfire shooting sparks into the sky.

In High School we located the hot mouths of boys,
broke up with ethereal Jesus—got drunk—

fish-tailed your Ford Pinto all over icy country roads.
I still have a Becks beer mug from those nights
clutching pencils on my desk.

And now we're thirty-three and now we live
in burnt-out mirror cities on opposite coasts—
escapees from the Midwest—and we are troubled
with migraines   husbands   lovers   Xanax   the scalding mouth of Jesus.
They scan us, take our blood, pronounce us "young-healthy."

They cannot find the day Andrew began puncturing his veins
with heroin nor the night Suzanne swallowed handfuls of pills
in that safest of all places—the Midwest—
that mother-fucking pure place—
and now your brother is in jail: you lock him in,
lock him out—turning the key over and over.
And my sister unravels from the dead each
time I return to Illinois.
I carry her burial garments with me
—wrapping and unwrapping—and so
we shoulder our heavy miracles like a burden,
and are making new plans to drive cross-country—
to meet at the edge of the Grand Canyon.
Last Christmas you went ahead of me chain-smoking the whole way—
only four quarters for one diet Pepsi—desert sand
powdering your bleached blond hair. You arrive
alone and wait for the blow-torch of morning
lighting each fissure of rock, layer after layer—
but all you see is the prairie fire lighting
the ends of your fingertips, your hair, your house,
our mothers' sad promises, and the new friend
who walked across the smouldering fields just to meet you.

Ice Skating With the Ophthalmologist's Children

The lake wore a monacle of rime.
Lid or lens;
Patch or pince-nez?

We did not know
So we scraped the snow
From the frozen window through which we peered
Into the depths of the underwater world.

Were the fish frozen too?—
Fish we had caught last summer and un-
Hooked
Because we could not bear to slash
Their corniced scales
And close the desperate gills—
Dark pink fringed gills
Gaping for deep underwater air.
Were they staring back at us?

We did not know,
But walked upon frozen green-black water
And pushed the snow away;
Did not get rid of the snow;
But carved a huge semi-
Circle wound upon the white lake;
A wound through which we cast our wonder—
Dormant—
Drowned in ice,
Poised for thaw.

We wanted to finish the other half,
But I noticed the backs of the little boys' ears
Turning dark pink;

And a scalloped moon,
Like a shovel's edge,
Clanging against the ice sky.

"Love, and a Bit With a Dog"

—from "Shakespeare in Love"

"Soul, one's life is one's enemy.
As the small children learn, what happens
Takes over, and what you were goes away."
—Robert Pinsky

It's one of those "call the lawyer-out-to-lunch—neurologist's-on-vacation—parents-out-to-sea—
soon to be X-wife" mornings.
One of those mornings when, without warning, they remodel the hallway with crowbars and sledgehammers and I have a migraine and I'm all out of painkillers and going to be thirty-five years old this year any morning now.
One of those mornings when they serve the divorce papers while they remodel the hallway as they do a credit check on me and my soon-to-be-X-husband who caused a pile-up on the Schuylkill just the other morning. It's one of those "let's drive 90 miles per hour on the Schuylkill Expressway mornings—weave in and out of traffic on Easter morning" mornings.
One of those "demolish another car and walk away invincible—'see, I've totaled another car I still love you and it's not yet noon'" mornings.
It's one of those "thank God Sue gave me a one-half pound solid milk chocolate Easter bunny named Zachary" mornings.
One of those "pay the phone bill—pay the mover—take the belligerent cats to the vet—write a nice letter to the new boss while they remodel the hallway'" mornings.

It's one of those mornings when my X-lover—X—admit it—X—has been reading the obits again—he's really getting up there—any day now—any morning—Will it be heart congestion? Will it be cancer?—When am I moving back?—When?—He wants to know the date the time what to bring over as he walks down the street with his cellphone, pacing around the block in his Mephistoes—turns a corner—loses reception.

Whatever happened to mornings when me and Laurie and Bob and their German shepherd Rikse had Godiva chocolates and coffee and just a little poetry to begin the day? And Bob and I argued poetry and journalism as Laurie and Rikse listened, beautiful and perplexed.

Whatever happened to me and Klaus-Peter in his Porsche racing Laurie and Bob and Rikse in their white Volare station wagon off the 34th Street exit ramp to Chinatown for Dimsum every Sunday morning? Last I heard, Klaus-Peter totaled the Porsche on the Autobahn, Bob's brother was killed on the Anaheim two Christmases ago, his sister has cancer, Laurie and Bob divorced, the dog died.

I wanted to tell the truth, but the facts were not the truth. I could explain the who, what, where, when, but never the why. Each defendant had a different answer—like snowflakes—each pattern unique, but fallen from the same sky. I played my part as journalist in the black and white grainy film of mornings at Criminal Courts, 26th and California. Dust particles dirtied shafts of winter light filtering down to the tile floor. Ten years of mornings ago.

And Laurie and Bob made wonderful food and didn't let me drink too much and calmed me with poetry and Billie Holiday. Six days a week there was murder, but Sunday there was love. They were holier, in their way, than any church I attended. And more than Jesus, they saved me. Mornings, I dreamed about beautiful wolves and woke up with an arm thrown around Rikse, because the sleeper-sofa was, after all, her bed. And she looked at me with the unselfconscious innocence that only animals know and thought, 'It's my small upset reporter friend sleeping in my bed again.'

I take a place behind the bullet-proof Plexiglas window, among Chicago's other journalists. I finger a hole in the shoulder seam of my jacket and look down at gray newsprint stains around the cuffs. I wonder why I'm wearing a linen suit in January. When I raise my eyes—there he is—a serial-killer, looking a little ordinary, a little dumb—looking more normal than the detective under questioning.

It's the shark tank dream, the blood tank dream, the shark tank dream again. They say: "if you pass the test no one else will have to take the test." They say: "be objective." They equip me this time—wet suit, mask and snorkel, fins. They hand me a spear gun. I'm lowered into a cylindrical glass tank— hovering a moment—a neoprene cupid come to shoot the shark through the heart. I make a small splash and heavy water suctions me under. Triangles of artificial light fracture the water into black and white curtains. The vibration of something large moves the water beneath me. Torque of cervical ligaments—back and forth—up and down—as my eyes search for the shark now blasting out of the shadows—pectorals pointed down, back arched—attack mode.

Instead of fear I think of language—how it evolved from math. Lists of flax; lists of sheep; pictograms of flax, sheep—ideograms; Pound's ideogrammatic method; Gilgamesh; Dead Sea Scrolls, and teeth like wedged cuneiform, row after row after row. I smash the butt of the spear gun against its snout, against its lidless eyes —smash it over and over. My mask fills with blood and water. I need air.

He turns another corner and finds my voice again. I picture him in the morning sun—wind lighting his curls, blessing him, almost, as he paces around in his loafers, wearing a suit coat over a T-shirt, cigar and paper clips in his breast pocket, collar turned up, holding a cell phone to his ear. I wonder what excuse he'll make this time for this version of love. I remember the first time we met—when all he was to me was the dearest friend—dear friend. I remember telling him about Laurie and Bob and Dimsum Sunday mornings. I remember saying, "If Laurie and Bob can't make it—who can?" And Laurie and Bob have not made it. He asks, "Oh, what are you crying about this time? What are you crying about now?" And I say, "Nothing really. Just a dog."

My Syria

for Stephen Berg

Musician of words you are my Syria.
I am through with hatred;
Ambitions of hatred.
No one is going to win this war
Of words of love.
Your body is the only territory of God
I know; and, O, how I have fought,
And lost to mortality.
Kingdom of mayflies:
I would fight and die for that.
Remember how we loved?
No borders, vows, religions—
No headlines to stop us.
And then...

Everything

In this city
I found everything I've ever loved,
I lost everything I've ever loved,
And now I have only the river,
Which, some mornings,
Like this one,
Is enough.

I still have Washington Square Park,
Large stone sidewalks,
Bones of soldiers breaking underneath,
Mud and the gray March grass.

I had a husband once.
I had a lover.
And, in this city,
I almost had a child.
All gone now. Gone.

But I still have the bronze rain
And the silver Atlantic rain.
I still have my tears the ellipsis of rain.
There is still a bronze angel
Holding up the downtrodden at 30th Street Station,
Where I arrive
Where I depart.

Before the Strangling

for Leidy Bonanno, in memoriam

My hairdresser was the only man I trusted
to wave scissors near my throat, but when he asked,
"Are you ready to lose the gray?," I said,
"Keep the gray," which is not what I would have said
before the strangling.

Before the strangling I would not have seen
the caterpillar attached to my car door—
mistaking the Mazda for a red enamel tree.

Or, if I noticed the caterpillar, I would not have been
astonished by its long white hair, nor by its colossal struggle
to summit my car—a fire-engine red Everest—
each foot-pod a suction cup of hope or adventure or desire
to ascend and conquer,
before the strangling;

Nor would I have worried that the caterpillar had strayed
from the park and was lost. And if—before the strangling
of a friend's daughter—who looked like my own daughter—
I had noticed the caterpillar and its Herculean
journey up my car door,
I certainly would not have offered a twig
to the tiny being who lifted its shiny black head
hypnotically toward the miniature wooden bridge.

I would not have "kept the gray" and
I would not have numbly stood there gently
coaxing the skeptical caterpillar onto the twig,
nor been oblivious to the segmented queue of SUVs
whose drivers honked and wrestled for my parking space—
ignoring their curses and waving fists—
as the caterpillar reluctantly climbed onto the twig,
which I carried back into the park
laying it at the roots of a sycamore.

Gray House

Mom was a housewife—the wife of a house;
Dad was a pilot grating against the ceiling.
He methodically consumed supper—
His spatula-tongue licking clean each aspiration
From the bowl of her heart.
Her eyes—black Brillo pads—scraped
Across his steel gray eyes blank.
Her forked words, his metallic silence,
Stabbed me like blunt butter knives.

House   House   House
Red house   blue house   yellow house
(with plastic flamingos ducking their pink heads in the grass)
Blended into a gray house when I ran.
I was running away from house,
But only got as far as Jojo Garberino's.

Jojo and all the Garberinos
Sat hunched around the TV set
Watching a dinosaur step on houses.

The picture reflected upon my T-shirt in achromatic light;
They watched, with innocent delight,
The dinosaur's lumbering movements as it mechanically crushed houses—
Red house   blue house   yellow house.

Jets, like toys, buzzed around the anachronistic beast
Pumping benign bullets into its bloodless flesh,
Dodging the blunt sweep of its claw,
But one jet was caught and clamped inside.

Jojo tried to explain that it was dead now—
That all the dinosaurs had died a long time ago—
And all the Garberinos nodded.

But that night, ducking beneath the covers,
I knew there was one left—
I could feel the weight of its dull foot
Descending upon my house.

Absolute Ceiling

The Earth is not a sphere, but an ellipsoid,
Precisely, it is a geoid—
A little fatter around the equator
Like most Americans.
Asphalt melts beneath the putty steps
Of our heavy, slow migration.

We cannot lose our collective weight.

It is not gravity
But the micro-gravity;
Not gravity,
But micro-gravity. The Micro-gravity Task Force
Has formed a Committee to study the problem.
They've written a rainforest of inter-office memos.
They shoot Winnebagos into Space. They're doing
The best they know how.

It is the late night ocean—
A screen of black sea black sky separated
By a thin white membrane
Of waves occurring fractally
Motivated by gravity.
The Earth's shape apprehends me.
I feel the movement of tectonic plates.
My footprints form fossils in the sand.

Tonight three cosmonauts
Missed their trajectory
Beyond Absolute Ceiling.
A pumice of weightlessness refines their bones to dust.

It is not life
But the little life;
Not life, but little life.
It is plankton and phytoplankton and diatoms

Swimming in their silica pillbox skeletons.
It is blue-green algae, photosynthetic bacteria—
Things we cannot see but know we breathe into
The twin-mirror tree of lung and brain.

It is not the nation;
But the planet;
Not the nation, but the planet turning
In its tear-shaped exo-pelagic envelope
To the music of the spheres.
It is Russians drowned in space and phytoplankton—
Cosmonauts in their diatomic capsule as lost
And little as a single cell in the wide black singular sea.

Not the nation, but the planet;
No longer the nation, but the planet,
Because the earth is not a sphere but an ellipsoid—
Precisely, it is a geoid.

Medical Earth

"Sit on my finger, sing in my ear, O little blood."
— *Ted Hughes*

That morning the virulent sun infected the whole sky
And the river infected the roses in my neighbor's garden.
The sun tossed light like confetti—purple, pink, orange—
Over the whole city. My wet hair froze in spindles
Around my head as I stormed down the street—
A parade of one.

I arrived at work two hours early and Isaac,
The small, Black doorman, who doubled as a preacher,
Let me in without a question—
No free sermons, no advice—
Just a look that meant to hold me together:
My starched suit clung to my soaked skin
Like bandages to Lazarus on razor fire.

I marched past a deadpan repetition of empty offices,
Found my desk, and started writing with both fists.

*

One of my co-workers, not my favorite,
Was dying of cancer. It seemed too corny.
One day walking up the stairs on my coffee break,
She caught up with me, grabbed my elbow, and said,
"I'm going to die,"
As though we were in the center of a deep pool
And she had suddenly forgotten how to swim—
Wanting me to hold her head above water.

*

We made our living reading about dying.
We were medical editors—oxygen-free radicals—
Separating and regrouping throughout the day
In our honeycomb of orange office cubicles.

At lunch we shocked each other with gross photos
And prurient stories that formed like a bolus in our throats.
At night we dreamed in tongues with words
Too foreign to be human.

We were all somatic—all called in sick
With retrovirus; malessesia fur fur
With fungemia; otitis media with effusion—
No common colds for us.
We had been scanned, all blood tested
For every possible disease.

But we were professional
Technic analysts of language,
Transmembrane signalers—correcting
Death's clinical grammar,
By moving cursors on a screen.

They said we did not need to understand
What we were editing. And we did not understand
What we were perfecting;
Not even after one of our own was diagnosed;
Nor after they fired her for missing too many days;
Nor after her last, routine phone calls;
Nor after she died and the company refused
To give us time off to attend her funeral.

They gave me her empty office
And a fear of death that ruined for me
The fact that I was alive.
She was the one who had died,
But I was the one who had been removed—
Traversing a new territory
Where ribbed clouds formed like hives
In the lungs of the sky,
And looking at that sky was like looking
At ocean waves from the bottom up.
My mouth watered for air
I could neither drink nor breathe.

City Bird Sursum Corda

If you ask
They will tell you—
Between beaks full of flat bugs
Pried from car grilles—
They will tell you.

Framed
In the diamond shaped gaps
Of steel link fences:
They look for trees
In a concrete world.

Plum feathers
Shrug off rain
As they huddle together on sidewalks
chanting in harsh iambics
The marriage of grief and gravity
Consummated in hollow bones.

How do I explain the Holocaust to my child?

Remedial God

Goshawk spies from a fence
On my way to the airport.

Algebra is a cadaver
Dissected by eager students.

Fear is the dogma
Of a remedial god.

The ice is thin
But I skate.

The ice is red
As tongues of mendacious archangels.

The ice resounds
But I skate.

Like a displaced goshawk
I fly.

Before Co-Dependency

for Laurie

Before AIDS; before we met
the wounded inner children
within our dysfunctional families;
before we feared death, taxes,
and the effects of the sun;
we lay on man-made blocks of stone
stacked against the shore of Lake Michigan.
Each hour we moved our bodies
where the sun was strongest,
where our shadows were smallest.
Each noon was like the last,
but lazier, longer.
We tended our tans, our hangovers,
the skin of our hearts so blistered, tender.
We chilled our passions in the lake's deep blue.
We were not afraid to sip
from the cup of shared lips.
The oil we smoothed on our skin was balm.
The color of our skin was gold.
Clouds, like columns, buoyed up the sky.
Wet curls circled our brows like wreaths
and the only word we knew was love.

Bone House Broken

"Ban-hus gebraec"
—— Beowulf

I stand before Monet's water lilies and know
I'm not Hamlet any more.
This "quintessence of dust" is my brave blond sister—
horse-tamer with gray eyes. This moment,
here, she will die young. I realize

all my life I thought I was Hamlet
—wise-crazy—commanding
away the poison poured into our family;
cutting it back with sword and skull
until no one remained standing.

I watch my sister, Ophelia, floating,
pale-hair braided with seaweed beyond me. As I reach
for her, woven steel chips the museum floor.
She picks up the sword where I drop it: Bone
house broken—roped to my heart of stone
slipping beneath Monet's lilies where I drown.

Compass of Fire

You met me at the train station
carrying a suitcase full of spiders.
All I wanted was a compass of rain.
Second hand of the antique clock
trembles like a divining rod.
And a red-tailed hawk—architect of air of dream—
lands on the weathervane outside
my office overlooking Independence Hall.

Meanwhile, heavy black rotary phones ring,
and ring, and Godblessit ring,
but I don't answer.
I cup a dead kestrel in my right hand.
In my left I raise a photo
of a doughboy wearing canvass spats.
And the photograph is burning.

[Meanwhile, the leaden rain
steams up hermetically sealed windows;
spools of typewriter ribbon unravel
from a retro Smith-Corona;
dirty-beige computers crowd the shelves,
jamb the doors;
wire spaghetti leads nowhere,
plugs into nothing;

one trillion consumers trill on the tip
of dysmorphic fingers].
But none of this matters.

What matters is my dream of a hundred butterflies
lighting on your shoulders like noon candles.

What matters now is transfiguration—
spiders into butterflies—
our daughter's translucent wings—

magnifying lenses of love—
invisible, clarifying.

What matters is 1914—
a half-breed from Oklahoma vomiting mustard gas
in a field in France; and the recurrent dream
of my Indian self stalking my English self.
When the spear's shaft splits my sternum
all I feel is an explosion of feathers.
Fingers sprout talons; hands, wings.
The spirit electric soars into stars, fire,
auroras of star.

What matters is the mosaic of watery glass
jigsawed together the same year my grandfather's lungs
fluttered for air like a vessel burst by a glass-blower to fragments—
Thierry, France. What matters
is the Parrish-Tiffany mosaic across the street from my office;

and especially the triangle of blue where mountains break:
never the same blue.
What matters is that I never let go of this photograph,
however hot and bright it burns:
compass of fire;
weathervane;
hawk rain.

Dream Garden

Out of a dry sky raining red leaves musk
leaves outside but windows raining leaves
dry but windows opening upon an autumn
garden ruined garden
the good government of trees
of sycamores
vellum sky sweating leaves diffuse
sun pointillist fog raining syc-
amores oracles
suddenly a hawk
snaps a shoulder blade of sky
slices through a cloudburst of leaves
badge of pain of hope reeling I
should be crying human tears salt
tears paper tears
droplets of red on red blood leaves
I should wear a city hawk on my shoulder I
remember when I loved hawks only nothing
but a dry sky autumn garden dream
garden hawk
garden.

Dream of Me

Condos now: the building
where I worked when
I was young. Oldest
publishing house in
America. Beds now,
instead of books; pillows
rather than towers
of paper. What
do they dream? Does ink
flow down the drain when
the new inhabitants shower?
Do they erase dust
instead of letters?
To be young,
to be young,
to balance the world
and its words
on my tongue.
Before computers
and the Fax machine:
What do they dream?
What do they dream?
Dream of me.
Dream of me
and my poverty.

Afraid to Pray

Dear God I'm afraid if I pray for my daughter's safety you'll blithely
allow her to get raped or abducted or crash on a highway
on a perfect summer day. Forget I mentioned my daughter. What daughter?

I remember how Anne Frank believed in the goodness of mankind.
I wonder how she felt the moment her diary was knocked from her hands,
because that's how I'm feeling these days: Like Job with post-traumatic

stress disorder. Don't worry God, I know you exist; but, I'm having some
serious trust issues. Maybe it began with that nightmare about my
mother shoving my grandmother into a swift-running river.

I jumped in to save her, and I saved her alright, but O the branches
and Kentucky mud stuck in our hair and mouths—the disbelief
in her eyes—and me having to tell her the truth.

Dear God if you made us in your likeness because you were
lonely then uh oh. I'm so tired of Nazis marching to the rhythm of my
        prayers.
I prayed that the love of my life would survive his cancer then he died on
        my birthday.

And for 30 years I prayed my x-husband would survive his insanity, but he
finally blew his brains out. I know there's a heaven because
I walked along a tightrope of Atlantic foam after Joel died and

a rainbow embraced the sun. The sky was timorous and thin
as an ear drum and I knew if I pushed with all of my strength
that the sky would burst and we would touch hands one last time.

I'm so tired of praying and getting punched in the gut. I prayed that
my parents would not sell my sister's black Morgan horse with the star
on its forehead, but they sold it alright and now she's afraid to love her own
        children.

I prayed that my parents would not sell the hand-built log cabin on the
      Indian
Reservation, but when they knew they could die without selling it, they
      sold it
alright and it was plowed under by the new owners along with everything
      in it

including a Bible my mother had placed just so. And they chopped down the
forest and threw my canoe in a dumpster. Now all I do is scour real estate ads
for log cabins on the Indian reservation. I've found a few places but they're
just not the same. Still,

I'd like to move back to the north woods and live in a cabin and pray to the
      lake
and the woods and the wolves. Like God the wolves would not answer my
      prayers,
but unlike God, by God they would listen for once and look me straight in
      the eye.

Skyward

It was a morning just like this
without a scar in the sky.
The hemlocks stood at attention.
Wrens formed notes on a wire.

Each neighbor's lawn was mown.
Each blade grew in its place.
Morning Glories saluted the sun,
and roses lit up my face.

Each "Stop" sign meant what it said,
and every church wore a spire.
All the dogs were walked and loved.
My thoughts hummed like a choir.

It was a morning just like this
when wings dropped like a sword;
and every door revealed a world
I never knew before.

The Boy Who Loved Planes

"All you have to do
is just sit there" — my husband
used to say about my
fear of flying. Odd,
I only had this fear while
married to him, maybe
because he was the boy who
loved planes — so much that
he read "Air & Space" magazine
before sex. He was the 747
and I was the landing strip. Odd,
how just boarding a plane
felt like suicide to me: 'Who
in their right mind would agree
to enter an aluminum tube
and depart the Earth?' But,
this morning, at 36-thousand feet,
I am not afraid of anything
except betrayal, poverty, and loss.
Most of my worst fears have come true
and none of them, not one, on a plane.
Not a year ago, my Joel inserted
a Glock-9 into his mouth
and squeezed the trigger. I want
to tell him I no longer fear flying.
I want to tell him: "All you had to do
was just sit there — sit there
and listen to the clouds
sluicing around the moist Earth
as it rolled through the Milky Way.
All you had to do was just sit there
and watch the jewelled galaxies expand."

Dragonfly

Always love the dragonfly
More than river deep —
Iridescent wands of light
Balance around my feet

I balance there too
Deaf, dumb rocks
Mouths too heavy to speak

Balance there too
Immutable stones
Tongues too heavy to break

O turn in the river
August sun shivers
Cannot bear to keep

River wild
Stillborn child
Cannot sing to sleep

Stickball (or Why I Love You)

Because the fog this morning
reminds me of Amsterdam at midnight,
and the morning glories opening,
and our child holding a plucked flower,
waving it, twirling it, toward
what light there is.

Because of Columbine, Kosovo, and
whatever form terrorists assume—
flying monkeys from the Wizard of Oz.
Because you were born before TV,
therefore, before the flying monkeys;
and before Hitler bolted a rectangular
screen of hatred over his mouth
like a miniature TV guttering barbaric dreams.
Because his reach, however far, fell short of you.

Because the internet cannot change human nature.
Because Apollinaire knew the truth about speed
and where it really takes us
if we're not paying attention.
Because you stopped to play stickball
with some guys on the streets of South Philly.

Because our child arranged shells in a flower pot
as though they were flowers.

Because whales sleep upside-down,
undulating like exclamation points
in the book of the ocean.
Because of the ocean.
Because when I'm doing linear algebra
on my computer at work,
I am really plowing a field in Kentucky—
driving a team of Clydesdales—
row after row over the curved Earth
a hundred years ago.

Because you cannot change a light bulb.

Because having a child who is half-Jewish
has changed the texture of my dreams
from folded steel to willow petal;
has changed the smell of my dreams
from airplane fuel and cigarettes
to musty, dog-eared books
stacked in an abandoned farmhouse.

Because you will not board an airplane.

Because of intractable sadness
riding your bike to work each day.
Because you are everything I love
about the Twentieth Century,
and not one thing I hate.

The Unborn Dead

Today the unborn dead dress up as birds.
Today they abandon their cradle of sticks
and fly for the first time,
climbing down the sky
on a ladder of wings:

Like the young eagle who landed
five yards in front of me—
surprised I stood my ground
when all the geese flurried away—
surprised at the blackness of his own feathers—
as black as my lover's hair
or coal flakes on fire.
His thighs were thicker than my wrists
and stronger as he paced
across the marsh and paused to stare
over the broken, unforgiven,
glass of black water.

My whole life I have watched birds
through precisely cut lenses
and taken notes in perfect handwriting.
Today I had no binoculars,
no paper, no pen, and anyway,
my hands were powerless
even to wipe away the nuisance of tears.

For years I've watched vultures
slide across the sky on hooked wings,
and hoped, even pretended, they were eagles.

Today the eagle is here and I'm not ready.

After the Blizzard

I finally looked away
from the Middle Eastern
wars glittering
on my Apple. Nothing
like the polished rain
of Midwestern snow.
I had forgotten about
the certainty of blizzards.
I was raised in blizzards
before Apples; before
the sky-scrapers fell;
before suicide-bombings;
before the beheadings
of the truth-tellers;
before my child —
who scintillated
all my life like a
shower of diamonds, like
a Midwestern blizzard —
watched me ski
through towering forests
descending toward the frozen lake.
Look! She's pointing at me.
The snow-bowed branches
are her finger-tips trembling.
The arctic wind is her voice
speaking and believing in me
like snow's gravity:
"That's my mom
skiing through a blizzard

"That's Mom! — before
the glass-metal towers
broke all to pieces storming
down, down, around
her shoulders dropping;

her knees buckling.
That's my mother
before the Age of Terror —
that pregnant instant
before the airline passengers
understood
this was the last flight
of their lives.
That — is — my — mother
whose words are destined
to be chiseled
into the granite steps
of the university
that betrayed her clean,
white, drifting soul
where she skis
looking for and loving
only me."

The Absence of Trees

I miss the absence of trees
and the prairie's tall sky.

My Indian Self has finally killed
my White Self. Horse heart. Wolf eye.

I have dreamed about this
all of my life.

And just like the dream,
the instant the heavy spear

splits my sternum, a thousand
hummingbirds fly out, and up, and free.

The Richard Snyder Publication Series

This book is the 20th in a series honoring the memory of Richard Snyder (1925-1986), poet, fiction writer, playwright and longtime professor of English at Ashland University. Snyder served for fifteen years as English Department chair and was co-founder (in 1969) and co-editor of the Ashland Poetry Press. He was also co-founder of the Creative Writing major at the school, one of the first on the undergraduate level in the country. In selecting the manuscript for this book, the editors kept in mind Snyder's tenacious dedication to craftsmanship and thematic integrity.

Deborah Fleming, Series Editor, selected finalists for the 2016 contest.
Final judge: Andrew Hudgins

Snyder Award Winners:

1997: Wendy Battin for *Little Apocalypse*
1998: David Ray for *Demons in the Diner*
1999: Philip Brady for *Weal*
2000: Jan Lee Ande for *Instructions for Walking on Water*
2001: Corrinne Clegg Hales for *Separate Escapes*
2002: Carol Barrett for *Calling in the Bones*
2003: Vern Rutsala for *The Moment's Equation*
2004: Christine Gelineau for *Remorseless Loyalty*
2005: Benjamin S. Grossberg for *Underwater Lengths in a Single Breath*
2006: Lorna Knowles Blake for *Permanent Address*
2007: Helen Pruitt Wallace for *Shimming the Glass House*
2008: Marc J. Sheehan for *Vengeful Hymns*
2009: Jason Schneiderman for *Striking Surface*
2010: Mary Makofske for *Traction*
2011: Gabriel Spera for *The Rigid Body*
2012: Robin Davidson for *Luminous Other*
2013: J. David Cummings for *Tancho*
2014: Anna George Meek for *The Genome Rhapsodies*
2015: Daneen Wardrop for *Life As It*
2016: Pamela Sutton for *Burning My Birth Certificate*